KENNEDY
WITHOUT TEARS

The Man Beneath The Myth

B Y

TOM WICKER

Foreword by ARTHUR KROCK

Illustrations by BILL BERRY

———

WILLIAM MORROW & COMPANY

NEW YORK · 1964

. .

TO MY MOTHER

. . . and to all Americans

who loved John Kennedy

FOREWORD

THE human race has ever been plagued by a hunger for heroes, anthropomorphic like the gods among whom the ancient Greeks installed them. So they become legends when they die, some while they still are living. And the superior qualities that have made them heroes are lost for years and even centuries in the sentimentality of the legend.

When destiny decrees for the hero the martyrdom of violent death in the midst of uncompleted labors, the legend forms instantly. And unless its unreality is promptly pierced by the informed and objective evaluation of those who knew and appreciated the real man, he enters the fog of mythology.

So dense and clinging is this fog that American schoolboys only recently have learned that Abraham Lincoln was a professional who employed all the tricks of the political trade to get the Republican nomination for President in

1860. They remain generally unaware that Lincoln did not "free the slaves" by the Emancipation Proclamation; only those beyond his reach in territory still controlled by the Confederacy; that the Proclamation was a move of military strategy primarily designed to the winning of the War Between the States, not a compulsion of the moral conscience which made repugnant to Lincoln the institution of human slavery.

George Washington died full of years and glory, and human greatness and frailty, in his bed at Mount Vernon. But the legend he became in his lifetime denied the frailty. Generations of American schoolboys believed the truth of the fable about the cherry tree, and chanted with Washington's "biographer," Parson Weems, that the first President "could not tell a lie."

The myth had passed so long for history that in my own schooldays we solemnly debated whether Washington had intentionally tricked Cornwallis into believing the Colonials would not make their stand at Yorktown. And to argue the affirmative, even on the justification of essential military strategy, was to take the highly unpopular side.

In the following word portrait of John Fitzgerald Kennedy as he actually was, Tom Wicker has rendered the service to contemporary and future history of striking at a legend in the first phase of its mounting evolution. The truth explains what the gathering myth obscures—that Kennedy was endearingly and admirably human. That this was what drew to him the people of this nation and the world. That this was a principal source of the share of greatness which is his due.

What emerges from Mr. Wicker's profile is the natural, gifted, somber and witty, deep and superficial, uncertain and resolute political and private man that in combination was John Fitzgerald Kennedy. The book supplies for history the pedestal of a monument more lasting than bronze, far more expressive of the grace and strength and style of his personality and career than the Eternal Flame, and the airports, the bridges, the public buildings and geography to which his name has been given, which the author suspects would have "embarrassed" him.

I share the suspicion because, among Mr. Kennedy's endowments—rarely to be found in politicians and even rarer when they attain the Presidency—was the capacity for cold and critical self-examination. A sufficient example is Mr. Wicker's relation of how the President accounted for the rejection by Congress of his proposal to establish a Cabinet Department of Urban Affairs, while letting it be known and published that he planned to assign the office to Robert C. Weaver, a Negro. "I played it too cute," said Mr. Kennedy. "It was so obvious it made them mad."

Thus he would have understood the ready acceptance, by so many who had deplored his death as an irreparable tragedy to mankind, of the rapid transformation of the Kennedy to the Johnson Administration. He knew that the sense of loss is transient except among the few; and that, as Milton wrote in *Lycidas:*

> Fame is no plant that grows on mortal soil,
> Nor in the glistering foil
> Set off to the world,
> Nor in broad rumour lies,
> But lives and spreads aloft by those pure eyes,
> And perfect witness of all-judging Jove;
> As he pronounces lastly on each deed,
> Of so much fame in Heaven expect thy meed.

Arthur Krock

KENNEDY

WITHOUT TEARS

—

SHORTLY after President Kennedy was shot, the following inscription appeared on a plaque in one of the private bedrooms of the White House:

In this room Abraham Lincoln slept during his occupancy of the White House as President of the United States, March 4, 1861–April 13, 1865.

In this room lived John Fitzgerald Kennedy with his wife Jacqueline Kennedy during the two years, ten months and two days he was President of the United States, January 20, 1961–November 22, 1963.

Before many years pass, that deliberate linkage of two Presidents, that notice chiseled upon history by Jacqueline Kennedy, may seem as inevitable as the Washington Monument. Already, airports and spaceports and river bridges and a cultural center have been named for her husband. Six months after his death books about him, even phonograph records, were at floodtime; many more were being written or planned. *Profiles in Courage* seemed destined to be a perennial best-seller. It was almost as if he had never called businessmen sons of bitches, sent troops to Ole Miss, the refugees to the Bay of Pigs, or kicked the budget sky-high.

Thus, John F. Kennedy is certain to take his place in American lore as one of those sure-sell heroes out of whose face or words or monuments a souvenir dealer can turn a steady buck. There he soon will stand, perhaps in our lifetime—cold stone or heartless bronze, immortal as Jefferson, revered as Lincoln, bloodless as Washington. One can imagine the graven words on his pedestal:

Ask not what your country can do for you. Ask what you can do for your country.

What his country inevitably will do for John Kennedy seems a curious fate for the vitality and intensity, the wry

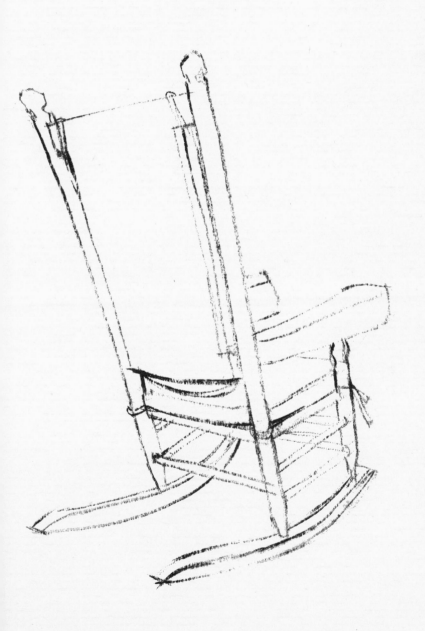

and derisive style of the man who was the Thirty-fifth President of the United States. His wit surely would have seared the notion of John F. Kennedy International Airport, much less Cape Kennedy—for this was the man who once told the great-great-grandson of John Adams, "It is a pleasure to live in your family's old house, and we hope that you will come by and see us."

One suspects the Eternal Flame might have embarrassed him as much as the Navy did that brilliant Pacific day when the strutting admirals put him literally on a flag-draped pedestal aboard an aircraft carrier while the band played *Hail to the Chief* and the jets screamed overhead on taxpayers' money; one of his favorite quips, after all, was that he had gone from Lieutenant J.G. to Commander-in-Chief without any qualifications at all.

I can almost hear that amused Boston voice inquiring, as he once did after reading a favorable Gallup Poll, where all those people who admired him so much were when Congress turned down his school bill in 1961. Staring from Valhalla at himself cast in stone in the middle of some downtown Washington traffic circle, he might well whisper to earthly passersby what he once told 12,000 Democrats in Harrisburg, Pennsylvania:

"I will introduce myself. I am Teddy Kennedy's brother."

And when children rise reverently in some future Fourth of July pageant to recite the chiastic prose of the Kennedy Inaugural Address—the stirring words that raced so many pulses among that "new generation of Americans" to which he appealed—some may recall instead the same rhythm, the same rhetoric, but different words and a more subtle imagination at work:

"We observe tonight not a celebration of freedom but a victory of party, for we have sworn to pay off the same party debt our forebears ran up nearly a year and three months ago. Our deficit will not be paid off in the next hundred days, nor will it be paid off in the first one thousand days, nor in the life of this Administration. Nor, perhaps, even in our lifetime on this planet. But let us begin—remembering that generosity is not a sign of weakness and that ambassadors are always subject to Senate confirmation. For if the Democratic party cannot be helped by the many who are poor, it cannot be saved by the few who are rich. So let us begin."

In much the same vein were Kennedy's remarks at a dinner of the White House Correspondents Association in April, 1962. The organization had just raised its dinner

ticket prices—and Kennedy had just forced the steel com-
panies to rescind a somewhat more important price increase.

"The sudden and arbitrary action of the officers of this
association," he said to the correspondents, "in increasing
the price of dinner tickets by $2.50 over last year constitutes
a wholly unjustifiable defiance of the public interest . . . In
this serious hour in our nation's history, when newsmen
are awakened in the middle of the night to be given a front
page story, when expense accounts are being scrutinized by
Congress, when correspondents are required to leave their
families for long and lonely weekends at Palm Beach, the
American people will find it hard to accept this ruthless decision made by a tiny handful of executives . . ."

Now a politician who could laugh at parodies of his
noblest speech and his moment of most spectacular success
—let alone make the parodies himself, as Kennedy did the
foregoing—obviously was something more intricate in life
than the mere sum of the virtues symbolized by the Eternal
Flame: purity, steadfastness, warmth, light. A President
delighted by the political caricature of Everett McKinley
Dirksen, but impatient with the solemn earnestness of
Chester Bowles obviously had a wide streak of Honey Fitz
down his spine; yet that same President, confronted with an

adulatory mob of hundreds of thousands of cheering Europeans, could not bring himself to respond with more than a halfhearted jab of the arm from the chest—something like a halfback straight-arming a tackler, apologetically. But let us not imagine that he was merely unemotional; those who saw it are not likely to forget his flashing anger when a reporter asked him at a news conference about two "security risks" in the State Department.

In the early days of Kennedy's New Frontier (there was bound to be something roguish about a man who could bring the Ivy Leaguers—and himself—to Washington with a slogan that evoked echoes of the Wild West, which appalled most of them), I thought Richard Nixon was perhaps a more interesting *man* than Kennedy. I thought Nixon was, as Conrad wrote of Lord Jim, "one of us." But Kennedy, I thought then, for all his charm and fire and eloquence, was a straightforward political man, who listened to his own rhetoric, contrived his "image" in the comforting faith that a statesman had to get elected before he could do anyone any good, and believed sincerely that his causes were not only right but actually offered solutions to human problems. I thought Kennedy had what someone has called the perfect political mentality—that of a football coach, combining the will to win with the belief that the game is important.

Now, I think that what Kennedy really had of that mentality was a rather peculiar form of the will to win. He wanted power, all right, but something more; "This ability," he once said, "to do things well, and to do them with precision and with modesty, attracts us all." It was a theme to which he often returned—the pursuit of excellence. And as the probability of his political canonization turns toward certainty, and the sad calcification of his humanity into stone and bronze continues, there is not much football coach in the man Kennedy who recalls himself to me most strongly.

If that human Kennedy still seems to me to have been altogether too detached and too controlled to have been, as were Nixon and Lord Jim, "one of us," with all those fascinating hesitancies and inadequacies and torments out of which literature is made, nevertheless he *was* a man "of few days and full of trouble," and for all I know he may even have played "such fantastic tricks before high heaven as to make the angels weep." But the statues will tell us nothing of that.

NOT many of them, for instance, will bear inscriptions drawn from his wit—that derisive, barbed, spontaneous wit, just short of mordant, that played so steadily through his speeches and recurred in such stable patterns of wording and attitude that it strikes me in retrospect as the true expression of a point of view, of a way of thinking not subject to time or circumstance or conditions.

It is astonishing, in retrospect, how constantly and boldly this Irish Catholic President, this young man so publicly committed to things like patriotism and public affairs, lampooned politicians, politics, notions, men, systems, myths, himself, even his church. When *The Wall Street Journal* criticized Nixon, Kennedy said, it was like *"L'Osservatore Romano* criticizing the Pope." And Speaker John McCormack denies that Kennedy called him "Archbishop"; "He called me 'Cardinal,'" McCormack recalls.

When the Vatican implied some criticism of Kennedy's campaign efforts to prove himself free of papal influence, Kennedy said ruefully to a pair of reporters: "Now I understand why Henry the Eighth set up his own church."

He and McKinley were the only Presidents ever to address the National Association of Manufacturers, Kennedy told that august body, so "I suppose that President McKinley and I are the only two that are regarded as fiscally sound enough to be qualified." And to the $100-a-plate guests at a glittering political occasion, he confessed: "I could say I am deeply touched, but not as deeply touched as you have been in coming to this luncheon."

In the spring of 1962, he returned from an Easter holiday and told the White House correspondents that he had been "back in touch with my constituents and seeing how they felt. And frankly, I've come back to Washington from Palm Beach and I'm against my entire program."

Not even the Kennedy family was spared its scion's irreverence. To a dinner of the Alfred E. Smith Foundation during the 1960 campaign, he remarked:

"I had announced earlier this year that if successful I would not consider campaign contributions as a substitute for experience in appointing ambassadors. Ever since I made that statement I have not received one single cent from my father."

Everyone remembers his remark, upon appointing Bob Kennedy Attorney General, that his brother might as well get a little experience before having to practice law; not so many heard him late one night at a Boston dinner last fall when he paid similar respects to the youthful Edward M. Kennedy:

"My last campaign may be coming up very shortly," he said, "but Teddy is around and, therefore, these dinners can go on indefinitely."

The Kennedy wit was so pronounced and so identifiable that it could be reproduced with near exactitude by Ted Sorensen, his speech writer. A deadly serious man, Sorensen's few recorded public jokes include one perfect specimen of Kennedy-style wit.

"There will be a meeting this afternoon of representatives from Baltimore, Atlantic City, San Francisco, Philadelphia, Chicago and other cities interested in holding the 1964 national convention," he said in a mock announcement to a Democratic party gathering. "The meeting will be held in Mayor Daley's room."

In order to laugh—as the Democrats did—one had to

know of course that Richard Daley was mayor of Chicago and one of the most powerful figures in the Democratic party—and that the competition for the convention was cutthroat. But Sorensen, as Kennedy always did, had tuned his derision precisely to his audience and the circumstances. The target was the situation—Daley's power, the party's foibles, the audience's pretensions. But whatever the situation, the *point of view* remained constant in Kennedy-style wit; it was the point of view that marked the man.

That point of view, as these few examples show, was a blending of amiable irreverence into a faintly resigned tolerance. It was a point of view that did not expect too much of human beings, even of its possessor; even less did it count heavily upon the wisdom or majesty of politicians; and often enough the political process itself was seen with frank disrespect. Perhaps a British M.P., but no American politician in memory except John Kennedy, would have been capable of the devastating "endorsement" of Senator George Smathers that the President delivered at a fundraising dinner in Miami Beach:

"I actually came down here tonight to pay a debt of obligation to an old friend and faithful adviser. He and I came to the Eightieth Congress together and have been associated for many years, and I regard him as one of my most valuable counselors in moments of great personal and public difficulty.

"In 1952, when I was thinking about running for the United States Senate, I went to the then Senator Smathers and said, 'George, what do you think?'

"He said, 'Don't do it. Can't win. Bad year.'

"In 1956, I was at the Democratic convention, and I said —I didn't know whether I would run for Vice President or not, so I said, 'George, what do you think?'

" 'This is it. They need a young man. It's your chance.' So I ran—and lost.

"And in 1960, I was wondering whether I ought to run in the West Virginia primary. 'Don't do it. That state you can't possibly carry.'

"And actually, the only time I really got nervous about the whole matter at the Democratic Convention of 1960 was just before the balloting and George came up and he said, 'I think it looks pretty good for you.' "

The audience was already in stitches, but Kennedy had saved the real barb of his wit to the last, for an astonishing punch line in which Smathers appears not only as a target but as part of an apparatus—the Presidency and its problems—that was in itself somewhat ridiculous in its pretensions:

"It will encourage you to know [Kennedy said] that every Tuesday morning . . . we have breakfast together and he advises with me—Cuba, anything else, Laos, Berlin, anything—George comes right out there and gives his views and I listen very carefully."

Nor did he stop with such small targets as Smathers. Composing a birthday telegram to his touchy Vice President, Lyndon Johnson, he once told a reporter, was like "drafting a state document."

When Prime Minister Lester B. Pearson of Canada arrived at Hyannis Port in the Spring of 1963, his reputation as a baseball expert had preceded him. The resident White House baseball nut was Dave Powers, an Irishman of jovial mien who could sing *Bill Bailey, Won't You Please Come Home* with marvelous vigah at the drop of a Scotch and soda. After a chilly Cape Cod dinner, Pearson followed Kennedy into seclusion, only to find it shattered by a summons to Powers.

"Dave," the President said, "test him out."

Whereupon Powers put the Prime Minister through an exhaustive baseball catechism, while the President rocked silently in his rocking chair, puffing on a cigar inscrutably, either measuring his man or enjoying the incongruous match—or both. Back and forth flowed the batting averages, managers' names, World Series statistics, and other diamond esoterica, until Mike Pearson had proved his excellence to the third decimal point of an earned run average.

"He'll do," Kennedy said then, with some satisfaction. After which he and Pearson hit it off famously and jointly equipped Canada with nuclear warheads.

PROBABLY the finest piece of work Kennedy did in his eight generally lackluster years in the Senate was his leadership of the fight against reform of the electoral college in 1956. He argued brilliantly for the system as it was and still is. His side prevailed for a number of sound rea-

sons, but not least because Kennedy succeeded in convincing enough Senators that, as he put it, "Falkland's definition of conservatism is quite appropriate—'When it is not necessary to change, it is necessary not to change.' "

That might almost have been Lord Melbourne speaking: *If it was not absolutely necessary, it was the foolishest thing ever done*, Melbourne said of a Parliamentary act. Indeed, Melbourne may have been in Kennedy's mind; for in the course of that brutal exposure of all his habits and persuasions to which Americans subject their President, it was to become known that his favorite book was David Cecil's *Melbourne*.

Probably no monument of the future will record that fact; yet it ought to give biographers pause. If the Kennedy campaign of 1960 meant anything, in terms of the man who waged it, it ought to have meant that Kennedy was a man who aimed to set the country right, who saw no reason it couldn't be done, who intended to let nothing stand in the way of doing it. The President who took office that cold day in January, 1961, saying, "let us begin," seemed to promise that the nation's problems could be solved if only enough brains and vigor and determination and money were applied to them.

Why would such a man enjoy reading of Melbourne, who believed government, in fact most human effort, was futile; who counseled, *When in doubt do nothing;* who said of a proposal to reform the English municipal councils, *We have got on tolerably well with the councils for five hundred years; we may contrive to go on with them for another few years or so;* and who thought the most damaging part of reform was that it aroused extravagant hopes that government and society—even men—might actually be improved.

But perhaps Kennedy was never quite the man the 1960 campaign suggested—just as Melbourne was not quite the fogy a few random quotations might suggest. Melbourne, in fact, as his biographer pictures him, was a man of immense charm and wit, great learning, considerable understanding of human nature, and remarkable courage in going his way—attributes that might be aspired to by any man. Certainly Kennedy possessed some of them and there is evidence to suggest that he shared to some extent Melbourne's skepticism about political and other human efforts at improving the condition of man.

The Kennedy wit certainly implies that he did. So did his

remarks on a famous television interview in December of 1962, when he reviewed his first two years in office.

"There is a limitation upon the ability of the United States to solve these problems," he said. ". . . there is a limitation, in other words, upon the power of the United States to bring about solutions. . . . The responsibilities placed on the United States are greater than I imagined them to be and there are greater limitations upon our ability to bring about a favorable result than I had imagined them to be. . . . It is much easier to make the speeches than it is finally to make the judgments. . . ."

And it might have been Melbourne speaking again when he said of his efforts to roll back steel prices: "There is no sense in raising hell and then not being successful. There is no sense in putting the office of the Presidency on the line on an issue and then being defeated."

A few months later, I asked Kennedy at a news conference if he would comment on what I said was a feeling in the country that his Administration seemed "to have lost its momentum and to be slowing down and to be moving on the defensive."

"There is a rhythm to a personal and national and international life and it flows and ebbs," Kennedy replied. He

even conceded—sounding not unlike Melbourne on the Reform Laws—that "Some of our difficulties in Europe have come because the military threat in Europe is less than it has been in the past. In other words, whatever successes we may have had in reducing that military threat to Europe brought with it in its wake other problems. . . ."

Later, Ted Sorensen was to publish a book that in its essence was a discussion of the limitations upon a President —the reasons why, as Kennedy wrote in a foreword, "Every President must endure a gap between *what he would like and what is possible*" (the italics are mine). Once again Sorensen had caught the spirit of his chief and reproduced it; politics was not after all simply a matter of brains and vigor and determination, or even money. Its events, life itself, flowed also from the contrary nature of men, the blind turns of chance, the inertia of custom. And in that same foreword Kennedy quoted Franklin Roosevelt as saying:

Lincoln was a sad man because he couldn't get it all at once. And nobody can.

On a more personal level, some who knew Kennedy well sensed something deeper than skepticism in him, though he was a private man who did not much reveal himself even to men who worked with him for years. He was absolutely fearless about airplanes, for instance, flying anywhere, at any time, in any weather in which he could get aloft, sleeping through anything, scarcely seeming aware that he was off the ground. Yet four persons in his family—his brother, his sister, Ethel Kennedy's parents—had died in aircraft accidents.

Kennedy sometimes discussed the possibility that he would be assassinated with members of his staff. They would be anxious to explain the details of security precautions to him, to show him that it was unlikely it could happen. "If someone is going to kill me," he would say, "they're going to kill me."

And one of those who was close to him believes that Kennedy bothered little about what he was going to do with all those years that presumably would be on his hands when he emerged from the White House at age fifty-one (assuming he won two terms).

"It didn't really concern him," the aide recalls. "He never thought he was going to live to be an old man anyway."

Y ET he had his imperatives. A man owed something to the public service. He had to be a patriot. He ought to be physically fit and courageous. (Good war records received special consideration on the New Frontier, and Dave Powers remembers that Kennedy once learned by heart the citation for a medal that had been awarded to General Douglas MacArthur.) A man's job was to act, not talk—to begin, to take the first step in a journey of a thousand miles.

Kennedy has been compared to Franklin Roosevelt and he liked to pose in front of an F.D.R. portrait. In fact, some of his qualities more nearly recall Theodore Roosevelt, the apostle of the big stick, the strenuous life and the bully pulpit. Like T.R., for instance, Kennedy had a perhaps undue regard for Harvard and a craving for its approval. The only election he ever lost was one of the ones he wanted most to win—his first try for a seat on the Harvard Board

of Overseers. He grimly ran again and his election to the Board was a cherished triumph. Like T.R., too, Kennedy fancied himself in the role of national taste maker—Roosevelt picked up Edwin Arlington Robinson and Kennedy adopted Robert Frost. Roosevelt let his rather rigid literary ideas get about and the Kennedys thought they ought to provide White House examples—Casals, Shakespeare and opera in the East Room—for the cultural uplift of the nation. Yet, after an American opera group had sung a scene from *The Magic Flute* in English, after a dinner for the President of India, Kennedy could confess to a group of guests: "I think they ought to sing it in the original language. It doesn't sound right any other way."

There is not much doubt that Kennedy's publicized delight in Ian Fleming's spoof-spy novels doubled Fleming's sales, although there has been no big run on Cecil's *Melbourne*. He kept green, graceful Lafayette Square in Washington from disappearing into the capital's Great Stone Face. One of his last interests was in a plan to redeem Pennsylvania Avenue from army-surplus stores, cheap steak houses and bumbling federal architects. But it was as if art and culture were in the National Interest, like the test-ban treaty and Project Mercury; and if Kennedy was an avid reader of history, he did not seem to suffer from a great personal involvement in drama, music, art. The movies shown in the White House screening room were often the commonplace of Hollywood, and, except in the East Room, Kennedy's favorite music was more nearly Sinatra than Schönberg. As President, his first venture to Broadway took him to the slick musical, *How to Succeed in Business Without Really Trying*. Once, when he had a group of newspapermen in his house at Palm Beach, I stole a look at a stack of recordings; the one on top was a Chubby Checker twist collection.

But the imperatives of taking part, of public service, seemed, like those that moved Teddy Roosevelt, to be genuine and even profound. To the Touchdown Club of New York, he quoted with obvious approval the rather fervent view of T.R. on the matter:

"The credit belongs to the man who is actually in the arena—whose face is marred by dust and sweat and blood . . . a leader who knows the great enthusiasms, the great devotions—and spends himself in a worthy cause—who at best if he wins knows the thrills of high achievement—and if he fails at least fails while daring greatly—so that his place shall never be with those cold and timid souls who know neither victory nor defeat."

Many times, he voiced a similar sentiment in his own words. Oddly, the man of detachment, of cool wit and ironic view, preached the "long twilight struggle" in which the most certain thing was that there would be "neither victory nor defeat." Yet, the man of commitment, of action, rejected with robustious Teddy the "cold and timid souls" who had no blood and dust upon their faces. And another quotation he liked to throw at university audiences was the rhetorical question of George William Curtis of Massachusetts:

"Would you have counted him a friend of ancient Greece who quietly discussed the theory of patriotism on that hot summer day through whose hopeless and immortal hours Leonidas and the three hundred stood at Thermopylae for liberty? Was John Milton to conjugate Greek verbs in his library when the liberty of Englishmen was imperiled?"

To the students of George Washington University, Kennedy gave his own answer: "No, quite obviously, the duty of the educated man or woman, the duty of the scholar, is to give his objective sense, his sense of liberty to the maintenance of our society at the critical time."

But in the next breath he was telling the story of someone who went to Harvard years ago and "asked for President Lowell. They said, 'He's in Washington, seeing Mr.
Taft.' I know that some other day, when they are asking
for the President of your university, they will say that he is
over at the White House seeing Mr. Kennedy. They understood at Harvard, and you understand here, the relative
importance of a university president and a President of the
United States."

If that was a joke, it did not come from one who often
gave up "his objective sense, and his sense of liberty."
Honey Fitz would sing *Sweet Adeline* until his tonsils gave
out, but his grandson was never known to wear a funny hat
in public. It may seem a small point, but John Kennedy
maintained it literally to his dying day. On November 22,
in Fort Worth, he went through the Texas ritual of being
presented a cowboy hat—but steadfastly resisted the pleas
of two thousand Texans that he put it on.

"Come to Washington Monday and I'll put it on for you
in the White House," he joked. But even in that compara-
tive privacy, had he reached it, he would not have worn that
hat. The man of detachment had yielded himself enough;
he would make his little pushing gesture at the crowds, but

he would not wave his arms exuberantly above his head like Eisenhower, or thump his chest like Theodore Roosevelt.

So, despite their similarities, he was radically different from the ebullient T.R. Restraint was his style, not arm-waving. There was nothing detached, nothing ironic, about Roosevelt, who could say and believe it that in the White House "my teaching has been plain morality." Kennedy would never claim more than that he hoped he was a "responsible President"; he would not often speak on television because he believed people would tire of him and stop listening.

Sometimes it seemed he even thought of politics, the Presidency itself, as a sporting proposition. Kennedy never tired of exhorting college students to prepare themselves for the public service, but he was seldom stuffy about it. He did not propose, he told the University of North Carolina student body, to adopt "from the Belgian constitution a provision giving three votes instead of one to college graduates—at least not until more Democrats go to college."

As the campaign of 1960 wore on, the atmosphere around the candidate sometimes seemed almost like one of those parlor games the Kennedys played so often. "Tell me a delegate and I'll tell you who he's for," Kennedy would say to members of his staff, in his best Twenty Questions manner. "Give me a state and I'll give you the delegate breakdown."

The election was so close it inhibited Kennedy; he would point out how closely divided was the country at every opportunity. Yet, he could compare his own disputed election to the plight of a Notre Dame football team that had won a game by means some thought illegal. "And we're not going to give it back," he told the National Football Foundation.

Kennedy disliked the solemn ideologues and myopic Babbitts who crowd American political life—Senator Karl

Mundt of South Dakota, for instance—but he delighted in the skillful shenanigans of some who took the game of politics less seriously—even, in some cases, when the voters and taxpayers were taken too. With obvious relish, he once described the operations of the raffish but highly effective Senator Warren Magnuson of Washington as follows:

"He speaks in the Senate so quietly that few can hear him. He looks down at his desk—he comes into the Senate late in the afternoon—he is very hesitant about interrupting other members of the Senate—when he rises to speak, most members of the Senate have left—he sends his messages up to the Senate and everyone says, 'What is it?' And Senator Magnuson says, 'It's nothing important.' And Grand Coulee Dam is built.

The night before he died, Kennedy spoke in tribute to Representative Albert Thomas in Houston, Texas. Not the least of Thomas' achievements over the years had been the enrichment of Houston with federal investments; his most recent coup had been the somewhat controversial establishment there of the Manned Spacecraft Center. Kennedy recounted a bit floridly how Thomas had helped put the United States in a position to fire into space the largest booster rocket bearing the largest "payroll" in history. As the audience laughed, Kennedy hastily corrected the word to "payload."

That slip might have embarrassed most politicians, but it obviously struck Kennedy as funny. "It will be the largest payroll, too," he added, grinning, "and who should know that better than Houston. We put a little of it right in here." Wasn't that what made the wheels go round?

Kennedy laughed out loud when he heard that Everett Dirksen had said that one of his early economic measures would have "all the impact of a snowflake on the bosom of the Potomac." He once carried a letter from de Gaulle around the White House, pointing out its elegances to his staff. It mattered less who won or lost than how they played the game.

Even the selection of winners of the Medal of Freedom, a sort of royal honors list Mrs. Kennedy and the President invented, was not free in Kennedy's mind from the sporting balance of politics—you scratch mine and I'll scratch yours. When the painter Andrew Wyeth was selected, Kennedy —who had put up an early argument for Ben Shahn—decreed: "Next year, we'll have to go abstract."

One night on his plane, returning to Washington from a speech in Trenton, he talked about his love of boating with a group of us, and confided: "I'd really like to have that yacht Eisenhower laid up in Philadelphia [the old *Williamsburg*]. But he said he did it for economy reasons and if I took it out of mothballs now they'd never let me hear the end of it." That was how the game was played; all you could do was grin and bear it, and play the game yourself.

Thus, John Kennedy in his pursuit of excellence, his commitment to active service, spent a great deal of his short life playing and thinking politics—running and angling for office, first; pushing political solutions to social and economic problems, second. But that is not necessarily the same thing as being profoundly involved in politics; it is not the same thing as a belief in solutions or the efficacy of politics. Kennedy seemed sometimes to think of himself as taking the first steps he so often urged upon the country and the world; he would use politics, he would propose a program, not with much hope for either, but to raise a question, to start someone thinking, to bring a matter into whatever light there was.

One Saturday morning in 1963 in Los Angeles he appeared at the Hollywood Palladium to address a Democratic women's breakfast: it was the only time I ever heard

Hail to the Chief played with a twist beat. He was supposed to make "brief remarks"; instead, he plunged in his familiar machine-gun delivery into a half hour of Democratic party evangelism so impassioned and so portentous of phrase that some of my colleagues wrote that he had "kicked off his 1964 campaign." I was so stirred by the speech that I phoned The *Times* to hold space for the full text of it. It was a "major address," I assured my editors.

When the transcript came spinning from the White House mimeograph an hour later, I thumbed through it in search of those memorable phrases, those ringing pledges, those grand calls to battle, that had rung through the Palladium. I have that transcript before me now and it confirms my disillusionment; there was nothing there, nothing but rhetoric and delivery. We had seen a performance in which J.F.K. had been playing the game unusually well.

In 1962, Kennedy proposed a Cabinet-level Department of Urban Affairs. Robert C. Weaver, the Administration's housing chief, was to be its Secretary—the first Negro to sit in any President's Cabinet. The proposal was hailed as a political masterstroke. Who could vote, in effect, against Weaver except the Southerners? And who cared about them?

In the long run, a great many members of Congress voted against the proposal and it became one of Kennedy's most embarrassing defeats. Not long afterward, I asked him how it had happened.

He took a cigar out of his mouth and answered bluntly: "I played it too cute. It was so obvious it made them mad." In short, he had played the game poorly. I think he often did.

Even after fourteen years on Capitol Hill, he seemed both to overestimate the resentment of that body toward Presidential whip-cracking and to underestimate Congress's determination to influence Presidential action. Before an audience in Miami Beach from which he had little further to gain, the A.F.L.-C.I.O., he was so palpably bored, his speech was so blatantly routine and uninspired, that men of more objective political judgment might have booed him from the platform. He went into General Eisenhower's home county during the 1962 campaign and delivered a speech so demagogic and so extravagant in its claims for Democratic virtue and Republican sloth that even the General was enraged and promptly proceeded to emerge from retirement to campaign against him—a development that might have been politically important had not the Cuban crisis changed the whole picture in October. On his Western trip in the Fall of 1963—his last extended tour in the country—Kennedy looked and felt so out of place talking about conservation and nature and wildlife that the reporters following him gave him the nickname "Smokey the Bear"; it was reported by Pierre Salinger at Jackson Lake Lodge that the President actually had seen a moose from the window of his room.

Shortly after Kennedy's death, Carroll Kilpatrick and I visited J. Frank Dobie at the University of Texas and asked him what was the difference in Kennedy and Lyndon Johnson. Mr. Dobie knew Johnson well; he knew Kennedy only as most Americans knew him—as a voice on the radio, a face on the screen, a presence in the land. "Johnson is concerned with means," Mr. Dobie said at once, as if the contrast was obvious. "Kennedy was interested in ends."

A generality, perhaps, but near enough to truth to *ring* true, particularly as concerns Kennedy. He played the game as a political man had to, sometimes brilliantly, often with boredom and ineptitude. But it was not then that he stirred us. Even his memorable campaign of 1960, the finest exercise of his strictly political life, was not politics-as-usual; it was outside the ordinary rules, for Kennedy was a Roman

Catholic, an inexperienced younger man, something of an intellectual, who put little trust in traditional politicians, and relied instead upon his own men, his own techniques, his own personality.

Perhaps he had to move beyond the rules, get out of the game, before he really involved himself—and therefore involved other men. His trip to Europe in 1963 exhilarated him, for instance; he knew he had broken through the traditional wall of diplomatic niceties, spoken above the heads of politicians and governments, and he believed a new generation of Europeans had responded. At his death, his tax bill was mired in Congress, but its mere presentation may yet be the longest step toward lifting American economic policy out of the twin ruts of ignorance and cliché. His civil-rights bill was tardy and forced upon him, but he was the first American President to recognize in the outpouring of events a "moral crisis" in race relations. The long shadow of de Gaulle darkened his European policy, but he had proclaimed on both sides of the Atlantic a commitment to the interdependence of two continents. Nobody could say there would be no nuclear war, but he had taken the "first step" of the test-ban treaty.

That is what haunts me about Kennedy—not just that

he was a man of certain admirable visions, but that he had the kind of mind that could entertain vision, the kind of outlook that could put in perspective the gambits and maneuvers of the moment, see truly the futility of most means, the uncertain glory of most ends. Surely he was one of those men "educated in the liberal traditions, willing to take the long look, undisturbed by prejudices and slogans of the moment, who attempt to make an honest judgment on difficult events"; surely he tried to be one of those, to borrow his words again, who could "distinguish the real from the illusory, the long-range from the temporary, the significant from the petty. . . ."

And that is the real irony of John F. Kennedy's coming immortality. For when James Reston asked him in the Summer of 1961, during a long afternoon's talk at Hyannis Port, what kind of a world it was he had in mind, what vision he had of the future, John Kennedy—President of the United States for half a year, perpetrator of the Bay of Pigs, not long home from his "somber" meeting with Khrushchev in Vienna—could reply: "I haven't had time to think about that yet."

It is the classic story of the liberal man in politics. *I claim not to have controlled events*, Lincoln said, *but confess plainly that events have controlled me.* And perhaps it is symbolized in a compelling picture of Kennedy that comes to us from one of Washington's most imposing men.

It is a glimpse from the Cuban missile crisis of October, 1962, a period of great tension at the White House as throughout the world. The personage and the President were alone in Kennedy's oval office, discussing what in New Frontier jargon were known as "the options"; that month, the options were pretty grim.

Kennedy rose from his rocking chair, leaving his visitor seated on a sofa. The President went across his office to the French doors that opened on the terrace of the West Executive Wing. Beyond the terrace lay the famous Rose Garden, redesigned like almost everything else about the White House by the elegant stylists who had come to live there. But at its end still towered the famous magnolia planted by Andrew Jackson.

Kennedy stood for a long time, silent, gazing at the garden and the magnolia, his hands behind his back, the burden of decision almost visible on his shoulders. "Well," he said at last, "I guess this is the week I earn my salary."

The detached thinker had been brought to bay by the necessities of the moment. That questing mind with its sensitivity to the complexity of things, to the illusory nature of answers and solutions, had come to the moment of black vs. white. That derisive and worldly wit was stilled in the sheer responsibility of choice. Action and events had overtaken contemplation and vision, and Kennedy shared the plight of Melbourne: *I am afraid the question of the Irish Church can neither be avoided or postponed. It must therefore be attempted to be solved.* And for Kennedy, that fall, humanity itself was the question.

So with his football coach's will to win, with his passion for "the ability to do things well," Kennedy had had his dreams and realized them. But I believe he stood on the sidelines, too, even while the game was going on, measuring his performance, wryly remarking upon it, not much impressed, not much deluded. Perhaps he knew all along that events would control, action overwhelm, means fail to reach ends. "There stands the decision," he wrote, "and there stands the President." Sooner or later, they would be as one.

The decisions he made, the slogans he spoke—let them be carved on the monuments. But for me his epitaph is inscribed on Dave Powers' silver beer mug, the one John Kennedy gave him for his birthday last year. It reads:

There are three things which are real:
God, human folly and laughter.
The first two are beyond our comprehension
So we must do what we can with the third.

No one else at the White House, then or a year later, knew that the source of those lines was Aubrey Menen's version of *The Ramayana*. I could find the words in no book of quotations. The Library of Congress was not able to tell me who wrote them. It is not a commonly known verse or an ordinary thought. But Ted Clifton, Kennedy's military aide, recalls him writing down those words one spring morning, quickly and without reference to any book. He had them by heart.